JOHNNY GAUDREAU

HOCKEY SUPERSTAR

BY ERIN NICKS

First Edition
First Printing, 2019

Book design by Jake Nordby
Cover design by Jake Nordby
Photographs ©: Brett Holmes/Icon Sportswire/AP Images, cover, 1, back cover; Gerry Thomas/ NHLI/National Hockey League/Getty Images, 4; Larry MacDougal/The Canadian Press/AP Images, 7, 9; marinat197/Shutterstock Images, 8; Elise Amendola/AP Images, 10; Michael Tureski/Icon Sportswire, 13; Fred Kfoury/Icon Sportswire, 15; Anne-Marie Sorvin/USA Today Sports/Newscom, 16; Bob Frid/Icon Sportswire, 19; Jason Mowry/Icon Sportswire, 21; Lynne Sladky/AP Images, 22, 30; Robin Alam/Icon Sportswire/AP Images, 25; Randy Litzinger/Icon Sportswire, 27; Red Line Editorial, 29

Press Box Books, an imprint of Press Room Editions.

Library of Congress Control Number: 2019936726

ISBN
978-1-63494-098-6 (library bound)
978-1-63494-107-5 (paperback)
978-1-63494-116-7 (epub)
978-1-63494-125-9 (hosted ebook)

Distributed by North Star Editions, Inc.
2297 Waters Drive
Mendota Heights, MN 55120
www.northstareditions.com

Printed in the United States of America

About the Author

Erin Nicks is originally from Thunder Bay, Ontario. She has covered hockey for newspapers and many websites, including NHL.com, for the past 20 years. Her favorite players of all time are Bryan Smolinski and Dominik Hasek. She currently resides in Ottawa, Ontario.

TABLE OF CONTENTS

1 LAST-MINUTE MIRACLE

Johnny Gaudreau didn't need to look at the clock. He knew time was running out in the third period. Gaudreau and the Calgary Flames trailed the Anaheim Ducks 3–2 in a crucial 2015 playoff game.

The Flames had an empty net, giving them an extra skater. Gaudreau sped down the boards on the right side of the ice. When he reached the faceoff circle, he came to a quick stop. Then, with only 19.5 seconds remaining, he snapped a perfect wrist shot.

Gaudreau (left) battles for the puck during a 2015 playoff game against the Anaheim Ducks.

The puck blasted past Anaheim's goalie. Gaudreau had tied the game with a rocket to the top shelf.

Calgary fans went wild as the horn blared. Gaudreau raised his stick in triumph. Then he pumped his fist and skated into the arms of his teammates. The score was now tied 3–3.

The Flames went on to win the game in overtime. And they couldn't have done it without the man known as Johnny Hockey.

Gaudreau's teammate congratulates him after his last-minute goal.

GAUDREAU'S LAST-MINUTE GOAL

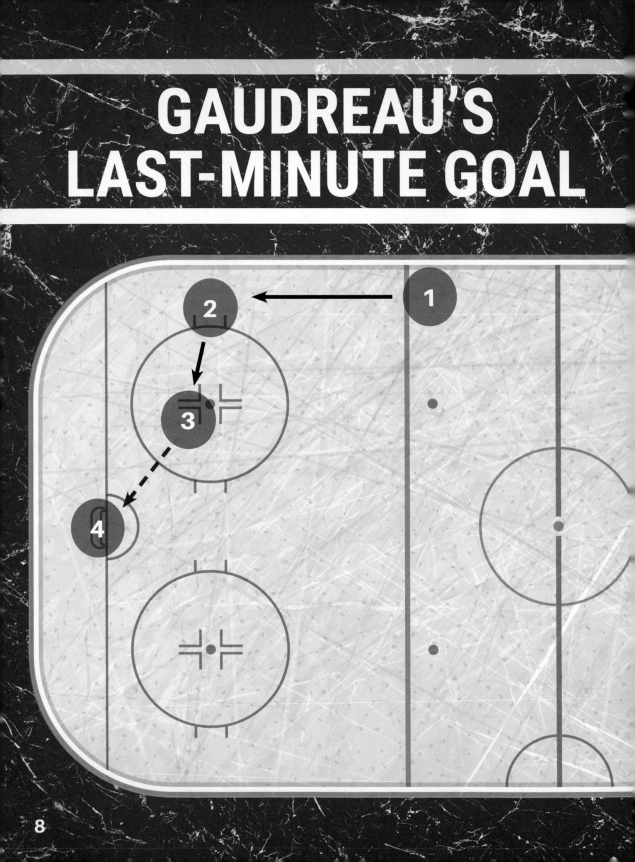

2 THE EARLY YEARS

Johnny Gaudreau was born on August 13, 1993, in Salem, New Jersey. He grew up in the nearby town of Carneys Point. Johnny loved hockey, but he was never one of the bigger kids. When he was a teenager, some teams cut him because he was too small. Even so, his father told him to keep playing. He said Johnny's talent was more important than his size.

In his final year of high school, Johnny moved to Iowa to play for the Dubuque

Gaudreau attempts to score against Providence College during a game in 2012.

Fighting Saints of the United States Hockey League. His talent earned him a spot on the league's all-star team. Better yet, Johnny helped his team win the league championship. He was also named Rookie of the Year for the 2010–11 season.

Standing just five foot six, Gaudreau didn't have the size of most other players. Even so, his scoring abilities stood out. With that in mind, the Calgary Flames selected him in the fourth round of the 2011 NHL Entry Draft. But Gaudreau wasn't ready for the big time quite yet. He joined the Boston College Eagles that same year.

The legend of Johnny Hockey began in Gaudreau's first season at Boston College. Scoring 44 points in 44 games was just the start. Gaudreau also played an important

Gaudreau tries to flip the puck past the goalie during a 2013 game against Boston University.

role in helping his team win the national championship in 2012.

With a little more than three minutes left in the third period, Boston College was clinging to a 2–1 lead over Ferris State. Gaudreau took control of the puck in the Eagles' zone. He flew down the center of the ice, crossing both blue lines. It took only one deke to skate past a Ferris State defenseman and get a shot off. With a quick switch to his backhand, Gaudreau flicked the puck past the stick side of the Ferris State goaltender. The Boston College fans went wild as the Eagles increased their lead to 3-1.

Gaudreau continued to improve during his next two years at Boston College. In the 2013-14 season, he scored an impressive 80 points. He also won the Hobey Baker Award. That trophy is given to the top

BOSTON COLLEGE BROTHERS

When Gaudreau was in his third year at Boston College, his younger brother, Matthew, joined the team. Johnny was already good enough to play for the Calgary Flames by this time. But he wanted to be on the same team as his brother, so he stayed with the Eagles for a third season.

Gaudreau looks for an opening against the University of Denver in 2014.

player in men's college hockey. There was no doubt about it: the young star was ready to turn pro.

3 WELCOME TO THE NHL

Johnny Gaudreau's first shot on goal in the NHL was one to remember. It happened in the final game of the 2013–14 season, when the Flames were playing the Vancouver Canucks. Early in the second period, Gaudreau skated into position in front of the goalie. Meanwhile, Flames teammate Chris Breen launched a slap shot from near the blue line. When the puck arrived, Gaudreau deflected it into the net. With that quick tap, Gaudreau

Gaudreau pokes in his first NHL goal.

became only the fifth player in NHL history to score on the first shot of his career.

Gaudreau learned plenty of valuable lessons in his rookie year with the Flames. To start with, opponents were not afraid to give him a hard time about his size. Gaudreau was five foot nine by this point, but he was still the little guy on the ice. During one game, Detroit Red Wings star forward Pavel Datsyuk leveled him with a monster hit. Gaudreau went flying and had to return to the bench to catch his breath.

Gaudreau knew there was a good way to handle insults about his size. The other players could keep taunting him, but he would keep scoring. The left winger went on to have a great rookie year. He became the youngest Flames player to score a hat trick since Joe Nieuwendyk in 1987. He was also the first

Gaudreau takes an acrobatic shot during his rookie season.

Flames rookie to score 50 points since Jarome Iginla in 1997.

By the end of his first season, Gaudreau had scored 64 points. He had also played in the All-Star Game. Best of all, he had helped Calgary return to the playoffs for the first time in six years. To cap off the season, Gaudreau was nominated for the Calder Memorial Trophy. This award is given to the league's best rookie. Gaudreau didn't win it, but he had plenty to be proud of.

In 2016–17, Gaudreau won the Lady Byng Memorial Trophy. This award recognizes great sportsmanship and great skill. It was the perfect fit for Gaudreau. He racks up the points, but he also plays a clean game. In fact, he only had four penalty minutes all season.

ALL-STAR PRANK

At the 2015 All-Star Game, Ryan Johansen of the Columbus Blue Jackets brought a young boy onto the ice during the breakaway challenge. Johansen helped the boy skate toward the net. As a joke, Philadelphia Flyers star Jakub Voracek asked Gaudreau to do the same trick. Voracek pretended to help Gaudreau skate, just like Johansen and the boy.

As a joke, Jakub Voracek helps Gaudreau skate during the 2015 breakaway challenge.

4 NHL SUPERSTAR

Johnny Gaudreau's skills have made him one of the biggest stars in the NHL. In particular, he's known for taking one-timers from the bottom of the faceoff circle. That's the same place where he scored his huge playoff goal against the Ducks during his rookie season.

Gaudreau can score on all four corners of the net and through the five-hole. As a result, it's hard for goalies to guess where Gaudreau is going to shoot. In the 2017–18 season, Gaudreau finished with

Gaudreau makes a move during a 2018 game against the Florida Panthers.

a career-high 84 points. His 60 assists ranked seventh-best in the NHL.

Gaudreau may rack up a lot of points, but not every shift can be perfect. Like any player, he has games when he falls into a slump. During these times, Gaudreau focuses on playing a defensive game. For a forward, that means skating smartly with the puck. Gaudreau focuses on not giving it away to the opponent.

Those stickhandling skills were on full display at the 2019 All-Star Game skills competition. Gaudreau blew away his opponents in the puck relay challenge. Gaudreau started the event by weaving the puck through several obstacles. Next, he hustled around a series of pylons. Then he lifted the puck through the slots on three barriers—and made it look easy. Finally, he

Gaudreau celebrates a goal against the Chicago Blackhawks in 2018.

flashed a big smile as he smacked the puck into the net.

Philadelphia is less than an hour's drive from Gaudreau's hometown in New Jersey. So when the Flames visited the Philadelphia Flyers in early 2019, thousands of people showed up just to see the local hero. And Gaudreau didn't disappoint.

In the second period, the Flames had a three-on-two breakaway. Gaudreau fed the puck to teammate Sean Monahan. Then Monahan passed it right back to Gaudreau, who blasted a one-timer into the net. The Flames went on to win the game in overtime.

By just about every measure, the 2018–19 season was Gaudreau's best yet. He led the Flames

RAISING MONEY FOR A CAUSE

For every goal Gaudreau scores, he donates $1,000 to charity. The money goes to KidSport, a local Calgary program that helps children in need by getting them involved in sports. Gaudreau also hosts a scholarship golf tournament in the off-season. The money raised goes toward the students of Gaudreau's high school in New Jersey.

Gaudreau dashes toward the puck during a 2019 game against the Washington Capitals.

in points, and his team had the best record in the Western Conference. Hockey fans seemed to agree that the future looked bright for the five-foot-nine winger. Gaudreau may be small, but his talent is huge.

TIMELINE

1. **Salem, New Jersey (August 13, 1993)**
   Johnny Gaudreau is born in Salem, New Jersey.

2. **Dubuque, Iowa (2010)**
   Johnny begins playing with the Dubuque Fighting Saints of the United States Hockey League.

3. **Saint Paul, Minnesota (2011)**
   Gaudreau is drafted by the Calgary Flames in the 2011 NHL Entry Draft.

4. **Boston, Massachusetts (2011)**
   Gaudreau begins his college career playing with the Boston College Eagles.

5. **Vancouver, British Columbia (April 13, 2014)**
   Gaudreau scores his first career NHL goal against the Vancouver Canucks.

6. **Calgary, Alberta (October 8, 2014)**
   Gaudreau begins his rookie season with the Calgary Flames.

7. **Las Vegas, Nevada (2017)**
   Gaudreau wins the Lady Byng Memorial Trophy at the NHL Awards ceremony.

8. **Tampa, Florida (January 27, 2018)**
   Gaudreau wins the puck control relay skills competition at the All-Star Game.

MAP

AT-A-GLANCE

Birth date: August 13, 1993

Birthplace: Salem, New Jersey

Position: Left wing

Shoots: Left

Size: 5 feet 9 inches, 165 pounds

NHL team: Calgary Flames (2014–)

Previous teams: Boston College Eagles (2011–2014), Dubuque Fighting Saints (2010–2011)

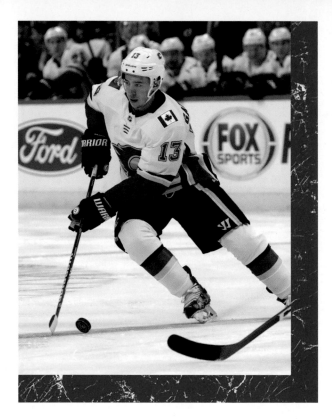

Major awards: Lady Byng Memorial Trophy (2017), NHL All-Rookie Team (2015), Hobey Baker Memorial Award (2014), Beanpot MVP (2012), USHL Rookie of the Year (2011)

Accurate through the 2018–19 season.

GLOSSARY

deke
When a player fakes a movement in a certain direction to confuse an opponent.

draft
An event that allows teams to choose new players coming into the league.

five-hole
The open spot between a goaltender's leg pads.

hat trick
A game in which a player scores three or more goals.

one-timer
A shot that a player takes immediately after receiving a pass, without controlling the puck first.

penalty minutes
Time that a player must spend off the ice after committing a penalty, leaving his team shorthanded.

point
A statistic that a player earns by scoring a goal or having an assist.

shift
The time that a player spends on the ice before needing a break, usually around 45 seconds.

slap shot
A shot in which a player winds up and slaps the puck with great force.

TO LEARN MORE

Books

Frederick, Shane. *Pro Hockey Records: A Guide for Every Fan*. North Mankato, MN: Compass Point Books, 2019.

Hall, Brian. *Sidney Crosby: Hockey Star*. Lake Elmo, MN: Focus Readers, 2018.

Peters, Chris. *Hockey's New Wave: The Young Superstars Taking Over the Game*. Mendota Heights, MN: Press Box Books, 2019.

Websites

Boston College Eagles Official Site
https://bceagles.com/index.aspx?path=mhockey

Calgary Flames Official Site
https://www.nhl.com/flames

Johnny Gaudreau's Goals for Kids
https://goalsforkids.ca/

INDEX